Unofficial Roblox Story

Diary of a Roblox Noob: Fortnite

Robloxia Kid

Contents

My dearest fans
and reviewers:

YTAHA
Coolalto940
Diamondminer168
Dragonfire
Tobi Salami
Ellen Henry
Natalija F.
JU

THANK YOU!!!

Entry #1:

Fort Bummer Shall Not Fall!

"All right everyone! Brace yourselves! Those monsters are advancing towards us! Positions everyone!"

We all heard the voice of Sergeant Jonesy booming across the fort. He just had the kind of voice that could easily echo through the hall. The sergeant also had a commanding presence that instilled fear in all of his troops. I guess he had to have that kind of intimidating authority to take down the monsters from the storm.

"This is going to be a big one! Eagle Eye

detected that horde coming towards us, and we've got to hold our ground!"

The whole hall erupted into activity. Everyone started running towards their positions around the fort. It was a beehive of action, and I wasn't about to get left out.

"Come on, Noob! Move!"

It was Urban Assault soldier, Headhunter. Don't let her good looks with her ponytail and shorts fool you. She was as tough as anyone in the whole unit. With a name like Headhunter, you knew that she meant business.

"Wait! I've never been into battle before!"

She ignored my pleas and tossed a bolt action rifle my way.

"Look sharp!"

I barely managed to catch it. The weapon

was so heavy in my hands, and I had never seen any weapon like it before, at least not from where I came from.

"This gun is so heavy! And it's not blocky like the other guns I've held before. Then again, I've never been in a real battle with so many monsters before in Roblox!"

Headhunter scowled at me and shook my head.

"This ain't Roblox, honey! This is Fortnite!"

"But..."

"Look! If you don't move now, you'll be Husk food! Now go!"

That was enough of a motivation for me to get moving, wherever I had to go. I would soon get even more motivation to get moving, and it wasn't from Headhunter.

There was a high-pitched sound that echoed

all over the hall. The noise was deafening. It resembled some kind of sharp, high-pitched scream. Once it sounded, the windows around the hall were instantly shattered. I covered my ears from the painful noise, and I could barely move. I could see that the squealing sound had the same effect on some of the other soldiers.

"It's a Lobber attack! Come on, Noob! You have to get moving!"

I was on the ground, covering my ears. I could barely hear Headhunter speaking. To be honest, I could only tell what she was saying because I was reading her lips. The screaming sound was deafening and echoed everywhere. It was so loud and piercing that it made it almost impossible to even move. I don't know how Headhunter managed even to stay standing and maintain her balance. She was indeed a well-trained soldier, I guess.

"I can't get up! The noise is too deafening!"

Headhunter said something that I really didn't hear now, and she picked me up. I was still clutching that rifle she tossed my way. This lady was really fit, and could probably lift a tank.

She carried me up and began to run. She didn't get far when I saw what appeared to be a fiery meteor falling from outside. I would later learn that it was a flaming skull bomb. This was the weapon of choice of the Lobbers, and a high-pitched wail was what often came before they came crashing down.

Headhunter hadn't gotten far when the flaming skull landed with terrible effect. There was a powerful explosion, and I thought that the entire hall had been engulfed in flame. Headhunter fell to the ground, and I rolled on the floor.

"Headhunter! Are you okay?"

She had taken a nasty tumble, and I honestly thought that she was done for. Well, I was wrong.

"I'm fine, but I can't carry you like that anymore! Come on, Noob! Move, or get cooked alive!"

There were smoke and fire everywhere. It was tough to just see in front of me. Somehow, I managed to get up and start moving. I guess I was motivated precisely by what Headhunter said. It was move or get cooked alive. I would prefer to choose the former.

The whole hall seemed to be engulfed in flames, but we managed to keep one step ahead of all the flames. Headhunter was running like crazy, but I somehow managed to keep up with her.

"Don't stop and keep moving, Noob!"

No argument here. We kept running until we reached the end of the hall. There was a door in front of us. Headhunter kicked the door open, and we managed to get out of that burning hall.

We made it to another area in the fort. Fort Bummer - yeah, that was the name of the fort. Chalk that up to Kyle, the Base Constructor's strange sense of humor - was a massive structure that you could easily get lost in. The fire was still raging in the hall, but there were already several constructors pouring inside with fire hydrants and anything that could possibly contain the blaze.

"Come on, men! We've got to put that fire out, or at least try to contain it from spreading!"

It was Kyle himself, and he was right in the middle of the blaze. Kyle was a portly sort with a thick mustache and beard, but with a ready smile for anyone. Kyle was probably the friendliest of the troops to me when I somehow ended up in the middle of all of this. There was no smile on his face now, and he was all business. He had to be, as that fire was really burning.

"Come on men, pour it on!"

"Headhunter! Good to see you're still in one piece. And it looks like you've saved Noob, as well."

It was Sergeant Jonesy. He stood over Headhunter and me and cut an imposing figure despite all the chaos that was raging all around.

"I did, but I don't know how long I can keep doing it."

"The lady's got a point Noob! Start moving that behind of yours because we ain't messin' around just to keep ya safe! This whole place is about to come down, so you'd better help out now!"

I heard the gunshots firing all around me. There was gunfire everywhere, and even a few explosions, definitely enough to make my ears ring. It was unusually harsh considering that I was no soldier at all, until now.

"W-what?! Help out? But how?! I'm not used to fighting!" I screamed out.

"Just fire your rifle, soldier!" Sergeant Jonesy commanded.

I took a good look at the heavy, iron bolt action rifle that Headhunter tossed at me earlier. It was a heavy weapon, and I had no idea just how smart it was to carry around something this cumbersome, but I had no choice. Beggars can't be choosers, right? I'd honestly prefer to have a cheeseburger on hand right now instead of a weird looking rifle, but I didn't wanna be monster meat either, so I just pulled the trigger and closed my eyes. The sound that followed was so powerful that it seemed a lot worse than the lobber's high pitched screaming. I actually went deaf for a few seconds because of how loud the gun was. Note to self: war is NOT fun.

"Keep firing, Noob!"

It was Headhunter. She handled herself very well amongst all the chaos, and I knew that this wasn't her first time. Nope, she didn't look like a doofus (like me) when in battle. I kinda felt embarrassed having her around me, so I felt I needed to kick things up a notch. This time, I aimed the powerful rifle at a monster that had just gotten inside the fort and pulled the trigger. The rifle let out a powerful, focused laser beam of pure energy and hit the monster straight on its chest. The creature flew across the entire fort, and it's body squarely hit one of the fort's hard walls.

"Ouch." I thought to myself.

The sound of the rifle also wasn't as loud as the last time, and it gave me the feeling that I was actually kind of getting the hang of this.

"That's it! They're almost retreating! Keep 'em out and make sure they don't come back!" the Sergeant shouted out. The rest of the troops inside the hall responded by wildly firing their weapons at the creatures who had made their way inside the fort. Bullets, gunfire, lasers, arrows and other piercing bullets flew through the air like fireflies on a damp night. It was getting crazy, and I ran towards the nearest desk for cover.

"Man, things are getting pretty crazy in here! Oh, what am I gonna do? What if one of those things manage to get me? How on Earth did I get myself into this mess?" I asked myself.

I closed my eyes and tried to remember, but everything was just an empty haze in my head, and I couldn't retrace what had happened no matter how hard I tried.

I was startled awake by the sound of glass shattering into thousands of pieces followed by menacing footsteps that were headed in our direction. I knew it only meant one thing: more monsters.

"Reinforcements! Hold fast, everyone! Hold fast!" Sergeant Jonesy said. He was obviously doing his best in trying to rally his troops, but the numbers were just not in our favor. There were way too many monsters coming in at once, and I had a feeling that Fort Bummer was about to collapse at any minute.

"What a bummer!" I thought to myself. Pun intended.

"Keep them back, guys! And where the heck is Noob?!" Headhunter cried out.

I poked my head out of the desk for a few moments and caught a glimpse of a small, yellow bus through a window just outside of the fort. The image of the bus suddenly snapped my brain into action, and I began to remember bits and pieces of just how I actually got into this mess.

Entry #2:

The Purple Storm.

It was a beautiful, warm summer day in Robloxia. The birds were chirping, the kids were playing, the leaves were... well, green, and the sun was shimmering. Yep, this was precisely the kind of day you'd probably have dreams about, and everything was just picture perfect. Well, almost everything, actually.

"Ah! I love this weather! Couldn't think of a better way to start my day!" I told myself.

Everything seemed to fit in so well, and I was just doing what I did best that day: being me!

I was thinking about some cool stuff to do on that day in Roblox Vehicle Simulator when suddenly, I saw something that was very, very startling, to say the least.

"What a great day! The wind is warm and refreshing, the sun is shining, and the sky is... purple?"

I caught a glimpse of the sky that had a strange, bright purple color. The rest of the sky seemed normal, but there was a weird part of it in the distance that appeared... well, purple. There was no other way to describe it, really! The sky was purple! What was going on? Was the sky sick? If I had a giant thermometer, I would have thrown it straight up at the sky to check its temperature. It just didn't make sense, and of course, being the curious guy that I was, I just had to know what it was all about.

"What's going on? I've seen a lot of storms

before, but nothing like this!"

I made my way to the parking area to get into my totally awesome ride. My car looked like some kind of a vintage hotrod with a huge engine and really slick looking decals on the side, but I didn't know just what it was called or how it worked. Hey, I wasn't a car guy, you know? If a car looked cool and moved fast, that was good enough for me! And I also wasn't about to check out those purple clouds on foot, no way! That would take too much time. Besides, I like to ride in style.

My friend, Randy, just happened to have been in the parking lot that same day. He was working on his car as always, and I thought he might have had some idea about why part of the sky was purple. Yep, that was Randy for ya. Half of the sky turns purple, and he still continues to work on his car. I bet Randy drank engine fluid instead of water whenever he got thirsty.

"Hey, Randy!"

Randy turned his head from his engine and looked at me. He waved his hand and smiled, and I waved back, of course, being the good friend that I was.

"Randy! What'cha working on now?"

"Nothing you'd probably understand," Randy said jokingly.

"Of course! Cars have never been my style, dude!"

"So how come you drive an X1 6 liter V8 eng-"

"Blah, blah, blah, I have no idea what you're talking about man. Hey dude, listen: have you noticed the sky lately?" I asked him.

"The sky?" Randy said. He seemed genuinely confused and started scratching his head.

I placed my palm on my face and pointed at the faraway portion of the sky that was purple.

"Whoaaaah! What is that?"

"Pretty sure you would have noticed that if you weren't working on cars all day, Randy."

Randy laughed and placed his hand on my shoulder.

"Hey, what can I say? I'm a car guy, eh?"

"I just don't get that part of you Randy. Anyway, you have any idea what that be?"

"Dude, if I knew, I would have told you about it earlier. Nope, no clue."

Both of us started staring at the purple sky and wondered what could have caused it.

"Do you think it's a storm?" Randy asked.

"Yeah, I thought about that earlier... but seriously, since when have you ever seen storm clouds that are colored purple?"

Randy shrugged his shoulders and smiled.

"Maybe you should go check it out!"

"Actually, I was thinking the same thing..."

Randy grabbed a large bucket of gas that had been modified to fit into custom gas tanks. My hot rod had a weird looking gas tank, and Randy's custom gas bucket was a perfect fit.

"I'll fill her up dude so you can take a closer look. Just make sure to tell me all about it when you get back, okay?" he said.

I hopped in my car and looked back at Randy. I raised my hand up and gave him a thumbs up.

"Will do!"

I inserted my slick, golden key into the ignition slot and turned the small, golden nugget. The engine suddenly roared to life, and just like that, my hot rod was ready to go. I placed my foot on the iron gas pedal, and the car started moving. I went towards the direction of the purple sky and didn't look back.

"Now let's see what we have here…" I thought to myself as I drove through the roads of Vehicle Simulator at 150 miles per hour. Yep, you heard that right. My car goes that fast. What can I say? Randy is a genius at modifying these babies!

Seconds soon turned into minutes and minutes turned into hours. I had felt like I was driving for what seemed like an eternity. I had already gone past the city limits, and soon enough, I found myself driving in the middle of the desert. It actually felt like the purple sky was trying to get away from me, and I was starting to get concerned about the amount of fuel I still had left on my hot rod.

"Come on already! Why can't I just get to the center?!"

A few, brief moments later, the clouds started swirling all around me. The sky was now an almost full shade of purple, and I couldn't even see the city in the distance. I was out in the middle of nowhere, and in the middle of a purple storm cloud. "Great going, Noob." I thought to myself. This was way closer than what I originally had in mind.

Just as I thought that things couldn't get any worse, my car started grumbling. I knew it only meant one thing: I was out of gas!

"Aww no! Not now!"

I stepped out of my stationary hot rod and placed my foot on the middle of the desert sand. The clouds were all still swirling above me, and I suddenly saw something in the distance that made my heart race faster than my car.

"I-is that a... t-tornado?!"

And it wasn't just some ordinary tornado, oh no. It was a purple tornado, and it was heading straight at me! I could see that it was moving pretty fast because I tried running away from it but to no avail. It was still heading straight at me like a bull with a bullseye set on my back. A few moments passed, and I could already see the violent vortex of purple winds engulf my hot rod in the distance.

"My car!" I cried out. I kept running, but I already knew it was too late. The car was definitely the least of my worries that time, and just getting out of this tornado alive would have been a miracle in and of itself. The vortex had engulfed me in its violent winds, and before I even knew what was actually happening, I was already twirling madly one thousand feet up in the air!

"Arghhh!" I cried out, but I knew that there was nothing that could save me now.

Nothing but a flying, giant, yellow bus.

Yep, you heard it right. Instead of landing on the hard, desert sand where I would have splattered like a tomato, I instead landed on the roof of a giant, flying yellow bus.

"W-what g-going o-on?!"

Suddenly, I felt the grip of a person's hand on my wrist, and it pulled me inside one of the windows of the bus. I could barely breath as the powerful winds almost sucked out all of the oxygen inside of me, and I collapsed instantly when I crashed into the bus.

"He's fainted! Somebody got a medkit in here?" a voice shouted out. I didn't know whose voice it was before, but now I knew exactly who it belonged to. It was Sergeant Jonesy.

"I think I can help him out, Sergeant! I have some Slurp Juice right here!"

It was Headhunter's voice now. I could barely see anything, and I was fast losing my consciousness. She pulled out what appeared to be a small jar with some blue, strange looking liquid and had me drink some of it. To my surprise, it actually made me feel a lot better, and I didn't expect that some weird looking juice would restore my consciousness.

"W-what..? Where am I? What's going on?"

I could see clearly now, and I saw a pretty looking girl with a ponytail, a well built, muscular, blonde haired man and a big dude with a really thick mustache. I didn't know who they were then, but I got pretty acquainted with them as I spent more time here in the world of Fortnite.

"I think you just got pulled in from the tornado, little dude! Thank goodness you're okay!" Kyle said.

"Yeah, I think so... wait, where are we headed?" I asked.

"To the Battle Royale, son. You'd best gear up, now that you're here. I ain't pushin' you down through that window so get ready to fight." Sergeant Jonesy told me.

"Fight?! But I'm not good at fighting! I'm more of a persuasive dude!"

"Sarge, his readings are off the roof! He's full of the element we're looking for!" Kyle said excitedly. He was pointing a weird, metal device at me and I had no idea just what it was.

"Wait, wait! Element? Fighting? Tornadoes? What-"

"Everyone, brace yourselves! We're approaching another rift! This is it! Get ready!" Headhunter said as she jumped back onto her seat and strapped on to her seatbelt. The flying bus was now starting to shake violently, and I didn't like the feeling of turbulence when riding on a giant, flying yellow bus. I knew my questions had to wait, so I jumped onto a seat, strapped on the seat belt, held on to the rail and hoped for the best.

Entry #3:

Back To The Action!

"We're losing it, boys! Hold them off!"

Sergeant Jonesy's sharp voice startled me awake as it echoed throughout the halls of Fort Bummer. I looked around me and saw chaos all over; bullets, laser beams, and arrows were all flying around like a swarm of locusts that had gone mad.

"Stop daydreamin' kid and pull yerself together!" Jonesy snapped at me. His voice sent a jolt of energy throughout my entire body, and I willed myself to get up from the desk.

"Commander! We can't keep holding on anymore! The fort is gonna collapse, and we're losing men by the minute! There are too many darned monsters-"

Just before the foot soldier could even finish his remark, he was felled by a large flaming skull obviously thrown by a lobber. The situation was looking worse and worse by the minute, and the commander knew there was only one thing he could do.

"Everyone! Code Purple! Abandon the fort! Fall back! Fall back!" Sergeant Jonesy cried out.

Call me a coward if you want, but I agreed with Sergeant Jonesy's call. I mean, there were about a hundred monsters inside Fort Bummer, and who knows how much more was headed our way. In fact, if I were Sergeant Jonesy, I would've called off trying to protect the fort several hours ago! But the guy's got a heart of steel, and nobody can say he didn't try.

"Darn! I gotta get outta here!" I told myself. But just before I could even get up, I felt someone grab me and snatch me away like a sack of potatoes.

"Way ahead of you, kid!"

It was Headhunter. She sure had a knack for saving useless soldiers like me. I didn't really understand or remember just why they had prioritized saving me over other, stronger soldiers that they could obviously use in battle. I mean, I know I'm good looking and all, but to keep saving me from certain doom while risking their own necks? I don't know... it sounded way too generous of them. And I'd find out why soon enough.

Even after Sergeant Jonesy's command, bullet and lasers, flaming skulls and all sorts of projectiles were still flying through the air.

I wasn't sure if the soldiers didn't hear their leading officer or they just didn't care. Either way, Headhunter definitely made sure that both she and I were getting out of the fort in one piece.

Headhunter ran through the halls of Fort Bummer like a bird soaring through the air. I could barely see anything as she strode gracefully along the halls filled with hostile monsters and while the wind was pushing up against my face. And although I couldn't see anything, I could definitely make out what they were saying.

"Kyle! Move it! Fort Bummer's a goner! We've got to relocate!" Headhunter shouted.

"What? Again? Man, I spent weeks trying to perfect this place! It'll hold, it'll hol-"

"Move it, Kyle! That's an order!" Sergeant Jonesy said. I assumed he was fast behind Headhunter and in a matter of minutes, all four of us were almost at the exit of Fort Bummer.

"It's the exit!" Kyle shouted out.

"What about the other soldiers?" I said as I hung there beside Headhunter, her arm wrapped around my whole body.

"I already made the command! If they don't comply, then there's not much we can do!" Sergeant Jonesy said. I could tell that he was already beginning to tire out as he panted in between his words as he spoke. He was definitely well built just like all of the soldiers inside Fort Bummer, but there wasn't anybody as fast and as agile as Headhunter. It was like she was some crazy ninja or something.

And if Sergeant Jonesy was already getting tired, I could only imagine what it felt for Kyle doing all of this running. Kyle was kind of a big-boned dude, and he certainly wasn't as well built like all of the other soldiers in Fort Bummer. But he was their brains, so they definitely needed him on the team.

After tearing through a few more monsters that blocked our path, we finally made it to the exit. All three of the soldiers ran away from Fort Bummer as fast as they could, and I looked back and saw the fort begin to collapse. I really felt sorry for the other foot soldiers who didn't make it, but Sergeant Jonesy was right. They had a choice. They should've known to run when the fort was already giving way. We didn't have a choice, so we had to abandon the place.

"This should be far enough!" Headhunter said. She let go of my body, and I immediately plopped onto the hard, green grass like a pile of rotten fish meat.

"Ow! Couldn't you have gone a bit easier on the landing, lady?"

"And can I offer you a platter of our finest, freshly bakes cookies with that, sire? No, of course not! You should be thankful that we even saved-" Headhunter said sarcastically.

"That's enough Headhunter. I'm just glad all four of us made it out alive back there." Sergeant Jonesy's said with his stern voice.

I saw a relatively large figure in the distance that was fast headed our way. I could've sworn that it was a monster, but I didn't know just how wrong I was.

"G-guys... w-wait... up..."

It was Kyle. Boy, did he look like he just spent sixty hours in a hot sauna! I wasn't even sure why he wore such heavy and menacing looking armor. I mean, yeah, it looked pretty slick and all that, but shouldn't a guy like him just wear a tank top all the time? I cringed as I saw him get closer and closer to where we were. It was like he was going to faint on the spot in front of all of us.

"Nice to see you made it, Kyle." Sergeant Jonesy said.

Kyle didn't respond. He merely collapsed onto the ground from fatigue.

"Is he okay..?" I asked.

"Yeah. He's just not used to running really long distances, dear." Headhunter said.

I looked back and saw the fort in the distance, or at least, what was left of it. It had completely collapsed, and monsters were all roaming around in the area, scavenging food and resources. It was a tragedy, alright. What a waste of good pizza. Yeah, I'm pretty sure they had pizza in that fort. How else could Kyle have gotten so big, anyway?

"Damn. What a waste. And I thought we had already established a good base of operations. Didn't see that coming."

Sergeant Jonesy said.

"Sarge... why are we saving the world... shouldn't the bus... have taken us to... Battle Royale?" Kyle finally said after laying on the ground and panting for what seemed like hours.

"I'm not sure either, Kyle. The vortex probably misguided the bus, so we ended up in here. A shame."

"Vortex? Saving the world? Battle Royale? Whoa, whoa, whoa, hold up! I don't get any of this? Where are we again? And what on Earth am I doing here?"

Everyone turned their head at me and gave me a stared at me strangely. It was as if there was an octopus on my head or something.

"Wait... so you're telling me you don't remember anything?" Headhunter said, looking surprised.

"Well, I remember the flying bus and the purple clouds..."

"Yeah, it was something else alright. Never seen what happened to you before. Not in all my years of being a constructor, not once, man." Kyle said. He seems to have finally recovered from that long sprint and seems to have regained his old luster.

"I remember being pulled into then somehow landing on that bus. But none of it still makes any sense! Where am I? And how do I get back to Robloxia?"

Headhunter, Kyle, and Sergeant Jonesy looked at each other and didn't speak. I had a bad feeling about the expressions on their faces.

Entry #4:

No Turning Back.

"Hey? Guys? Uhh... How do I get back?"

"Lemme put it this way, honey... that might be a little difficult."

"Well, what's the problem? I saw you guys fight, if it's gonna be just a little difficult, then I'm sure-"

"Let me rephrase that: It's gonna be next to impossible." Headhunter said.

My eyes widened, and my jaw almost fell to the ground. I honestly couldn't believe what I was hearing. First, a weird purple cloud appears out of nowhere on a bright, sunny day, then I get pulled into a tornado and land on a flying bus, then suddenly I'm in this weird place where it's full of monsters, and now this lady is telling me that I can't go home? This day just keeps getting better and better!

"That flying bus you saw earlier; that's our only mode of transportation around here. When we fly through the sky, rifts caused by that same purple cloud sometimes appear out of nowhere and teleport us to other dimensions... like that place you're from, Robloxia. Thing is, we can't really tell how those rifts appear or when." Sergeant Jonesy told me sternly.

"Whoa, whoa, whoa! Wait up... so you're telling me that the flying bus was your car?" I was trying to resist the temptation of saying "Sweet!" because this day was anything but sweet.

"Yeah, I guess you could say that. We left it behind in the fort though so there's probably no way we can get it back. Kyle here could probably build one with the right resources... but we'd have to look around hard."

"The thing is, dude, the bus was supposed to take us to Battle Royale. But instead, we probably didn't see a rift coming, got transported to your world Robloxia and got transported back here in Fort Bummer. The rift pretty much just turned us around." Kyle said.

"Battle Royale? What's that? Sounds scary."

"Well, it kind of is, actually. It's an arena not too far from here where the only other surviving warriors in the world duke it out for money and resources." Headhunter explained.

"Whoah! Wait... survivors? Are you telling me that this whole world has been swallowed up by those monsters and that there are only a few people left?!"

"Pretty much. Everything was a lot better than it is now, actually. The whole world was normal... until that purple cloud you saw up in Robloxia appeared. Then all of a sudden monsters started spawning everywhere. They took down everything civilization had built from the ground up... and we're only one of the few remaining survivors who are putting up a fight." Headhunter said.

Suddenly, a wave of worry started to overcome my entire body. I wasn't sure how to describe it, but all I knew was that it felt pretty bad. I thought about all of my friends back in Robloxia, the life I had built there and the relationships I had established. What if this purple cloud just ends up taking all that away? Not good. Not good at all.

"Oh man! What if that purple cloud spawns monsters up in my world, Robloxia? That's some seriously bad news!"

"The only way to find out is if we can somehow get back there. But these rifts... we can't predict 'em. But rest assured that if the purple cloud does spawn monsters in your world, we will come with you and fight them all back."

Sergeant Jonesy's last remark made me feel a lot better. I mean, I knew I couldn't count on just three butt-kicking soldiers to take down an entire army of monsters, but seeing as how they fought so well back Fort Bummer, I was sure that the monsters in Robloxia would have something to worry about if they decided to invade. Add the fact that I could warn the others about the cloud ahead of time and you've got yourself an army that's ready to fight!

"I've got to get back soon so I can warn the others in Robloxia!"

"It might take some time before we can figure out how to spawn a rift. We haven't really understood the nature of these rifts or these monsters just yet. They're all relatively new to us." Headhunter said.

"Actually, there might be a way... it's risky but possible." Kyle said.

Everyone turned around and placed their attention on Kyle.

"I've actually been studying these rifts for quite a while now, and, to be honest, I think I might have a way where we can spawn a rift. Check this out..."

Kyle pulled out a strange looking device from his pocket that looked like a really, really small metal detector with weird meters all over it. It was the same odd looking device he used on me earlier when we were inside the flying bus. He hovered it around, and the floater on the meter was on "Empty." But when he pointed the device at me, it suddenly read "High."

"Okay... what is that supposed to mean?" I asked.

"This device is called an element detector. It can detect all kinds of elements in the world, but I've tweaked it so that it can detect what's known as the 'FKST' element."

"FKST? What's that?"

"It's a rare element that's only sometimes present here in our world in areas where the purple cloud isn't present. It's an unstable element that can be harnessed to create a weapon that can be fired onto the center of the cloud, permanently destroying it while opening up multiple rifts to different dimensions."

I pumped my fist up in the air and smiled from cheek to cheek. I almost wanted to hug Kyle at that moment.

"Well, why didn't you say so, dude? Then let's make that weapon of yours and get me back home!"

"I did say there were gonna be risks, though. We would have to gather enough materials to build the weapon, then extract the FKST from your body. Your home, Robloxia, is full of FKST, and since you're from that place, your body is full of the stuff as well. After we've made the weapon, we're gonna need to find a vortex; fight through hordes of monsters; enter the vortex and hope that we don't somehow die from its gravitational pull; fight even more monsters inside the vortex; find the center of the storm inside it; then fire the weapon onto the eye of the storm, ultimately destroying it permanently and opening up the hidden rifts inside it to other dimensions."

Kyle's explanation was a lot longer and more complicated than I thought. Even so, I understood what he was trying to say, and I realized it was gonna be a lot harder to get home than I thought. I started scratching my head.

"Oh-kay... well, isn't there a simpler way to spawn a rift?"

"As of now, that's the only way. It's risky like I said."

"Well, it's worth a shot I guess. I can't stay here forever! I've got to feed my cat back in Robloxia!"

Headhunter giggled at my remark, and Kyle flashed a smile. Sergeant Jonesy didn't react and looked like a statue made out of human flesh.

"One thing I don't understand though, guys... this Battle Royale thing you mentioned earlier... I don't get it! Why don't all of the survivors in this world just work together to take down the storm cloud once and for all?" I asked.

"Things aren't that simple, kid. Since the cloud came out, resources have been harder to get. Water supplies, food and the like, it's all hard to find here. People get desperate and selfish, everybody don't wanna share nothin', and in the end, trust gets harder and harder to establish. Battle Royale makes it easy: the team left standing wins and gets all the resources the others brought with them. It's not the best method, but it's one that I can live with." Sergeant Jonesy said.

"Oh, I see. That's pretty tough." I said grimly.

"Nah, don't be like Sarge over here dude.

He's way too serious; he doesn't know how to have any fun! You get used to it after a while." Kyle told me as he placed his arm around my shoulders. Sergeant Jonesy gave Kyle a threatening stare that would have probably melted a monster right in its tracks, but not Kyle. Kyle was a fun loving dude who knew how to have a good time, and I was starting to like him a lot. Plus, he was my only chance of getting back home.

"I'll take your word for it, Kyle," I said.

"Well, Kyle, what'll we need to get started on that cannon? We'd better get moving now if we want to take down that storm and send Noob back home." Headhunter said as she stood up and readied her rifle for action.

"That's the easy part..." Kyle whispered.

Entry #5:

Kyle's FKST Particle Cannon.

"We'll need a few shadowshard crystals and some bright core ore to make the weapon. I can use the current element detector I've already built and merge it with the cannon to draw the FKST element from Noob. I've already got the schematics to build this bad boy, I just need the crafting materials. " Kyle said.

"Where we gonna get those materials, Kyle?" Sergeant Jonesy asked. I was actually surprised that someone like Sergeant Jonesy didn't know where to get those materials, seeing as how he's the most battle-trained of the three. Then again, that's probably why they've got Kyle around.

"Husks and Lobbers, Sarge. Exactly like the ones that took down Fort Bummer. Bummer it got taken down earlier though... pun intended." Kyle said.

"Nice pun. We'd better get to work then, guys. And as for you Noob--" Headhunter said as she threw a small, pocket-sized pistol my way. I caught it easily, and it felt more like a cell phone in my hand than an actual weapon.

"Use that. Best weapon for beginners in Fortnite."

"Beginners? Now wait just a minute--"

I accidentally pulled the trigger before I could even finish my sentence and the pistol let out a powerful beam of energy that looked like a lightning bolt. I had pointed the pistol towards a tree while I was talking and the energy beam completely decimated it. In just a few seconds, the tree had dissipated into a pile of burnt ash.

"Ughh... on second thought, I love being a beginner."

If this is what they called a "beginner weapon" in this game, I cringed thinking about what other, more powerful weapons were capable of doing.

"You sure we can take down all those mobs-I-I mean, monsters all by ourselves? If we couldn't do it earlier, how are we supposed to do it now?" I asked.

"We don't need to go through the entire group. We just gotta kill a few monsters so we can scan their bodies if they were carrying any of the materials we'll need. Maybe a hundred and fifty will be enough." Kyle said calmly.

I was sure I heard him wrong, though.

"A h-hundred a-and f-fif--"

Headhunter placed her hand on my mouth and smiled before I could finish my sentence.

"Watch and learn, honey."

"Okay..."

And just like that, Headhunter, Sergeant Jonesy, and Kyle rush off back to the site where Fort Bummer once was. Headhunter moved through the air like a plane that soared through the skies, but that was typical Headhunter for ya. In a matter of just a few minutes, I could already see that they were back at the site and were already cutting through the monsters like a hot knife through butter. I stood up and leaned towards their general direction as to catch a glimpse of the action. I was tempted to grab some popcorn and a coke, but knowing Headhunter, she'd probably hit me in the head with the stock of her rifle if I did that.

I saw Headhunter blast a Husk with her rifle, and the bullet hit the creature straight on its arm. The Husk fell to the ground and writhed in pain, and Sergeant Jonesy delivered the final blow by blowing up the sad monster with a frag grenade. Other monsters that were close flew through the air like lifeless ragdolls, and shrapnel quickly spiraled in every possible direction, hitting almost all the other monsters within the vicinity.

Meanwhile, Kyle was just as busy as his two other comrades. He laid down what looked like a small decoy of himself on the ground, and it started emitting a strange, low-frequency sound that seemed to attract the other monsters. Kyle also laid down what looked like a small device that seemed harmless to the untrained eye.

"Come to papa..." Kyle whispered to himself. He quickly ran off away from the decoy as fast as he could and took cover behind a large rock.

The zombies came ever closer to the decoy, and the device suddenly blinked a red light thrice before exploding into a gazillion pieces. I've seen some crazy stuff in this game like laser beams, disintegrators, flaming skulls and the like, but Kyle's device was unlike any other. It exploded with real fury, and the blast effect had a strange, blue color. All of the monsters who were even remotely close to the decoy and the device were instantly disintegrated and turned into a pile of ash.

"Oh yeah! Score one for Kyle!" he shouted out loud.

But for every monster that Kyle, Headhunter and Sergeant Jonesy dispatched and killed, it seemed that ten more came to take their place. It looked like an endless horde of monsters were coming from the shadows themselves.

"They're too many!" Headhunter cried out as she blasted another Lobber with a rifle.

"It's alright! I think we've got enough! Just hold on!" Kyle shouted out. He quickly took out his element detector thing and hovered it over some dead Husks and Lobbers. That's when I noticed a big smile had come onto Kyle's face and I knew that he had enough materials to create this weapon of mass destruction. Kyle bent down and began picking up as many shadowshard crystals and brightcore ores as he could find and fit into his bag. After gathering quite a number of those strange looking ores and crystals, Kyle placed his two fingers on his mouth and blew out a loud whistle.

"I've got enough! Let's go!" Kyle said.

Headhunter and Sergeant Jonesy nodded their heads and took down any other monsters that were standing in their way before regrouping with Kyle. Bullets and laser beams flew through the air, and explosions dotted the entire area, but Headhunter and Sergeant Jonesy were too agile and dexterous to get caught in any of those. No way, they were battle-hardened soldiers who have seen way too many fights in their time here in Fortnite.

"Let's get back! Come on, there are more on the way!" Kyle said as he regrouped with Headhunter and Sergeant Jonesy.

All three of them made their way back to where I was, but the Husks were now hot on their trail. The Lobbers were now also firing flaming skulls at the three soldiers as they ran away from the ashes of Fort Bummer.

"The monsters! They're chasing us!" Headhunter cried out.

"They probably didn't chase us earlier because of all the chaos and all the other soldiers! But now, we're the only people in the entire area, so all of them are focused on us!" Sergeant Jonesy said.

"Thanks, Sergeant Obvious! Keep running, we'll outrun them eventually!"

Kyle's prediction didn't come true, however, as the three were already close to me and the Husks simply wouldn't give up.

"Dangit! How am I supposed to craft the cannon if zombies are stalking us like this? I need some quiet time in order to study the schematics and craft the weapon properly!"

I reacted to Kyle's plea and pointed the laser pistol that Headhunter had given me earlier on a Husk. I pulled the trigger, and a powerful beam of energy was released from its barrel. The Husk was struck by the mighty bolt, and I could've sworn I saw its bones for a moment like an X-ray before it disintegrated into a pile of burnt ash.

"Noob, nice shot! Quickly, we need to cover Kyle as he builds the cannon so we can end this storm once and for all and send you back home!" Sergeant Jonesy said as he turned around and punched another Husk flush on its face. The husk went down hard on the grass, and Jonesy fired a menacing bullet onto its chest, permanently ending it' reign of terror. Unfortunately for us, there were about a hundred more who were coming our way and coming fast!

"Kyle, we'll cover you! Stay behind and craft the cannon!" Headhunter said.

"Will do, ma'am!"

"Noob, we'll need another hand! Get your

rear in here and take out some Husks!" Headhunter commanded. I felt like my heart pumped straight through my chest after I heard Headhunter's command. I mean, it felt good blasting that Husk into a pile of burning flesh, but a hundred more? That's a little too much for little ol' me!

"Guys, I just need a few minutes! This won't take long!" Kyle cried out.

"I sure hope it don't, cause I don't know how many more of these things I can take out!" Sergeant Jonesy shouted.

Entry #6:

The Nameless One.

Just when the Husks and the Lobbers seemed to have the numbers on their side, a powerful gust of wind suddenly enveloped the entire area. Kyle was hiding behind a rock, so his schematics didn't fly off. Boy, was I glad that they didn't. They were my only hope of getting back home!

The wind seemed to get stronger with each passing second to the point that the trees themselves were bending out of shape. Headhunter and Sergeant Jonesy were now gripping onto twigs and rocks just so they wouldn't get blown away. The force of this wind really reminded me of the tornado that got me into this mess in the first place! I quickly hid behind the rock that Kyle was behind as fast as I could.

"W-what in God's name is t-this?!" Sergeant Jonesy cried out.

As quickly as the wind had arrived with no warning, it disappeared just as fast. The trees were now bent back into normal shape. Headhunter and Sergeant Jonesy had loosened their grips on the rocks and twigs that they hung onto. The Husks and Lobbers had also stopped attacking, and they merely stood there motionless as if time stood still for all of them except us.

"What's going on?" Headhunter said.

All of the Husks and Lobbers quickly fell to their feet and collapsed with no warning. Everyone, including me, was utterly dumbfounded by what we had just seen. The Husks seemed to show no sign of mercy or retreat, but after a powerful gust of wind, have now fallen lifelessly onto the ground.

"I guess... we won!" I said. Oh, just how wrong I was.

Standing in the distance was a dark, slim and pale figure. The menacing figure wore a strange mask with intricate etchings inscribed onto it. It held a long, razor-sharp katana that looked like it could cut through the rock that Kyle and I were hiding behind.

"Who's there? Who are you? Show yourself!" Headhunter cried out. She aimed her gun at the shadowy figure and right after she pulled the trigger, a kanai had suddenly jammed onto its barrel effectively stopping her rifle altogether.

"What--"

The shadowy figure seemed to have teleported right beside Headhunter and held his sword straight against her neck. One wrong move and Headhunter was definitely done for. Who the heck was this guy?!

"Who are you? Answer me!" Sergeant Jonesy demanded. His gun was also decommissioned as the strange man threw a silver pin that stuck to the side of Jonesy's shotgun. The pin glowed a scary bright red and the gun's barrel slowly started melting.

"W-what is this?!"

"Oh no, dude... this is not good. Not good at all." Kyle whispered grimly. It seemed that he was the only one who actually knew who the mysterious person was.

"Who is that guy?!" I asked.

"It's the Nameless One."

"The Nameless One? He should have called

himself Lame One if you ask me!" I thought to myself.

"The Nameless One, as the story goes, was a normal Ninja, just like any other Ninja-"

"Whoa, whoa! You mean to tell me that there are actual ninjas in this world? Sweeeet!"

"Yes, of course! What did you think? Headhunter got her training from a ninja!"

Now I knew just why Headhunter moved so quickly. But even her extreme levels of agility were no match for this Nameless One. If we even had a chance of getting out of this alive, we had to beat this somehow mean looking dude... and fast.

"Anyway, the Nameless One was an average ninja who accidentally fell into a rift here in Fortnite. I told you earlier, entering rifts is a risky endeavor, and he didn't have any protection to cover him, so he vanished for several years. Everyone thought he was dead... until many, many years later, a ninja bearing the same mask and the same weapon suddenly appeared and started leaving destruction in its wake. The Nameless One spares no one, not Husks, Monsters or Trolls or people. He, or whatever it is now, just kills everything it finds mindlessly."

I gulped in terror as I listened to Kyle's tale about the Nameless One. If this guy is really as good as Kyle says, then we were doomed.

But I wasn't about to let this guy stop me from going home! No freaking way! I thought about all of my friends back in Robloxia, and a rush of adrenaline just suddenly overcame me. Then I did probably the dumbest thing I've ever done... and that's saying a lot because I do a lot of, you know, silly things.

I stood up from the rock that we were hiding behind and pointed my laser pistol at the fallen ninja. I pulled the trigger, and a powerful boom echoed throughout the entire area, and a menacing bolt of lightning was headed straight towards the monster. Just when I thought that I had caught him by surprise, he suddenly held up his sword, and the energy bolt quickly followed the blade. The blade absorbed all of the energy from my pistol, and I suddenly realized that I had just made a big, big mistake.

"Uh-oh..."

Just before anyone could react, Sergeant Jonesy threw a powerful uppercut straight at the ninja's jaw. It seems to have hit the ninja's chin flush, but the Sergeant's hand suddenly slipped right through his face like he was some kind of ghost. The Nameless One then teleport to Sergeant Jonesy's side and kicked him straight in the gut before the poor soldier could mount any sort of defense.

"Ughh!"

Headhunter moved quickly as she leaped through the air and descended down on the Nameless One with a mean looking flying kick. The Nameless One again slips through her like a ghost and Headhunter's foot lands on the cold, hard ground. Just before Headhunter could even stand up, the Nameless One grabs her by the throat and tosses her aside like she was some kind of weightless ragdoll.

With Headhunter and Sergeant Jonesy down, it was up to Kyle and me to somehow, some way, defeat the Nameless One with the tools we've been given. I mean, if Sergeant Jonesy and Headhunter couldn't do it, what chance did we have against this monster?

The Nameless One now slowly turned his head towards me, and I suddenly felt a wave of fear overcome me. It felt as if I was suddenly paralyzed and couldn't even move my limbs, no matter how hard I tried. My mind was awake, but my body just wouldn't budge. Was this some kind of ninja spell? I don't know, and I was sure that this was going to be the end for me.

"No!" Kyle shouted. He threw what looked like one of his plasma bombs similar to the one he used earlier against the Husks and the Lobbers. The device exploded in the air just as it came in contact with the Nameless One and lightning bolts began to surge in different directions although none of them ever came in contact with any of us. The explosion seemed to have been compressed into a single small area, namely where the Nameless One was standing. It was actually a pretty cool sight to see, and it definitely looked like the eruption was enough to decimate anyone or anything.

Kyle and I cheered and gave each other a high-five. The worst was over! The Nameless One and the monsters that he took down with him were gone. Kyle stood up from the rock to check up on Headhunter and Sergeant Jonesy. It was pretty hard to see anything after the explosion had pushed up so many leaves, grass, dirt, and smoke everywhere. Kyle and I squinted our eyes so we could get a better look.

And that's when we couldn't believe what we saw.

"He... h-he's still standing!" I cried out.

Kyle rubbed his eyes just to make sure he wasn't seeing things. Yep, the Nameless One was still alive. And it looked like he wasn't even scratched at all.

"How are we gonna beat--"

The Nameless One teleported towards Kyle

and stuck him with a mighty blow using the handle of his blade before the poor guy could even finish his sentence. Kyle immediately fell to the ground from the force of the Nameless One's attack.

Kyle, Headhunter, Sergeant Jonesy. Everyone was down... everyone, except me.

I knew there was only one way to beat this guy.

"Oh please, Mr. Nameless One, sir! Don't cut me up into a million pieces, please! I'll be your minion, I'll follow you around and everything, just please, please don't hurt me!"

The Nameless One stood still and didn't respond to my plea of mercy. After a few seconds that felt like hours had passed, he raised his weapon straight into the heavens and prepared to strike me down with his sword. So much for that.

I closed my eyes and prepared myself for the final blow. I didn't know it was gonna end this way.

"Well, I guess I oughtta just count my blessings, right? I had a lot of fun while I was alive, made so many friends and had a great time! Goodbye, everyone!" I thought to myself.

The Nameless One struck me down with his sword, and I waited for it slice me in half like a loaf of soft, tasty bread.

Entry #7:

Into the Eye of the Storm.

Then suddenly, a miracle happened.

The Nameless One's seemed to have stopped, and it was like he was stuck in animation or something. His blade barely scraped the side of my hair, but it was definitely touching a part of me alright.

"Well, I guess you decided to change your mind about the minion thing, huh, Mr. Nameless One sir? Mr. Nameless One?"

I waved my hand around his face. Nothing. It's like time really stood still for this guy. It was similar to what happened to the Husks and the Lobbers earlier when they stood still for a few moments before collapsing.

"Wait, don't tell me... there's another ninja behind this dude who fell into a deeper rift and is about to kick our butts all over again?"

The Nameless One's blade suddenly glowed a bright purple and parts of it started to disintegrate. The Nameless One himself also began to dissolve into thin air.

"Whoah! What's going on?"

"Y-yeah, dude... It's just as I e-expected..." Kyle mumbled. He could barely talk as that strike from the Nameless One really knocked the breath out of him.

"Kyle!"

I rushed to Kyle's aid and helped him get back up on his feet.

"You okay? You took a pretty hard hit there!"

"Yeah, Noob. I'm gonna be alright. Anyway, it's just as I expected. The Nameless One is a ghost powered by the storm's rift energy. Your body is oozing with the FKST element since you're from Robloxia. And since the element FKST is the opposite of rift energy, The Nameless One simply disintegrated when he tried to strike you with his blade."

"Soooo... it means I'm better looking than him?"

"Pretty much," Kyle said.

"Anyways, it also proves another thing that I've been theorizing recently..."

"Which is?"

It was Headhunter and Sergeant Jonesy. They both definitely looked better earlier, but we were both glad they were still okay nonetheless.

"Headhunter! Jonesy! You're okay!" I said.

"That's Sergeant Jonesy to you, kiddo."

"Pfft. Whatever. Just glad to know you guys are okay."

"So Kyle, what were you gonna say?" Headhunter asked.

"My theory was correct! Since Noob's FKST energy repelled the rift energy emanating from The Nameless One, it means that we'll have a chance of getting to the eye of the storm without getting hurt. And check this baby out..."

Kyle bent over behind the rock and pulled up what looked like some techno space cannon pulled straight out of a Sci-Fi movie. All three of us gasped and stood in awe at its sheer complexity and... ah, shoot. Look, it looked really, really cool, okay? I mean, super, duper, Star Wars level cool.

"I'm assuming that's your FKST cannon? The one we'll use to draw out Noob's FKST energy and to deploy it on to the center of the storm?" Sergeant Jonesy said.

"Exactly," Kyle said with a smile.

And so we had everything we pretty much needed to save the world and send me back home. Kyle's FKST deployment cannon, Headhunter's quickness and speed, Sergeant Jonesy's battle experience and my... well, hey, if it weren't for me, then they would've never made that cool looking cannon, okay?

There was only one thing left to do... we needed to go inside of a vortex that spawned monsters. And that, my friends, is another story for another day altogether.

The End.

If you enjoyed this book, please leave a review on Amazon! It would really help me with the series.

Best,

Robloxia Kid

20867875R00052

Made in the USA
Middletown, DE
11 December 2018